DATE DUE

Basic Math

Adding and Counting On

Richard Leffingwell

Heinemann Library
Chicago, Illinois

Photo research by Erica Newbery
Designed by Joanna Hinton-Malivoire
Printed in China by South China Printing Company Limited

10 09 08 07 06
10 9 8 7 6 5 4 3 2 1

Library of Congress Cataloging-in-Publication Data
Leffingwell, Richard.
  Adding and counting on / Richard Leffingwell.
     p. cm. -- (Basic math)
  Includes index.
  ISBN 1-4034-8155-5 (library binding-hardcover) -- ISBN 1-4034-8160-1 (pbk.)
  1. Addition--Juvenile literature. 2. Counting--Juvenile literature. I. Title. II. Series:
Leffingwell, Richard. Basic math.
III. Series.
  QA115.L448 2006
  513.2'11--dc22
                      2006005175

Acknowledgments
The author and publisher are grateful to the following for permission to reproduce copyright material: Getty Images (Photodisc Red/Davies & Starr) p. **22**; Harcourt Education Ltd (www.mmstudios.co.uk) pp. **4–21**, back cover

Cover photograph reproduced with permission of Harcourt Education Ltd (www.mmstudios.co.uk)

Every effort has been made to contact copyright holders of any material reproduced in this book. Any omissions will be rectified in subsequent printings if notice is given to the publisher.

Contents

What Is Adding?

When you group things together, you are adding them.

Adding helps you find out how many things you have.

Pretend that you have 5 toy cars.

Someone gives you 2 more.

Put all the cars together and count them.

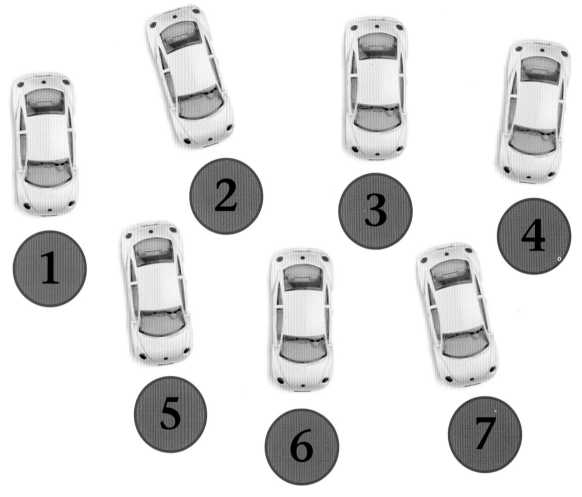

How many do you have?

$$5 + 2 = ?$$

You have 7 cars.

$$5 + 2 = 7$$

Adding Crayons

$$4 + 2 = ?$$

You have 4 crayons and get 2 more.

How many do you have when you add them together?

Count the crayons one by one.

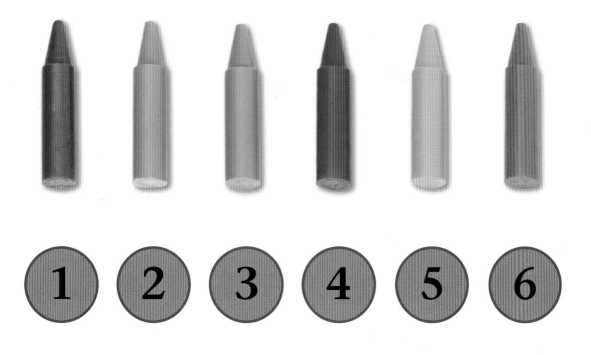

Counting everything takes a long time.

Can you think of another way to find out how many you have?

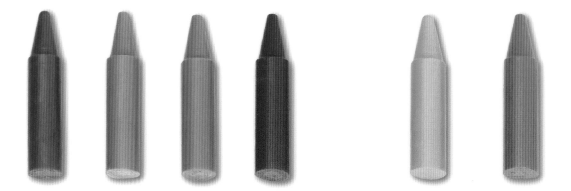

$$4 + 2 = ?$$

You started with 4 crayons.

You added 2 more.

Start at 4 and count on 2 times.

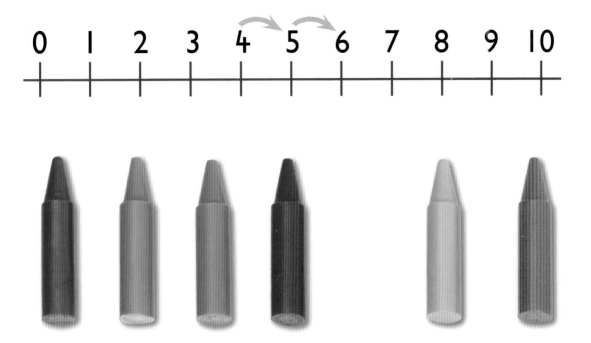

$$4 + 2 = 6$$

Starting with what you have and counting the new items is called counting on.

Adding Erasers

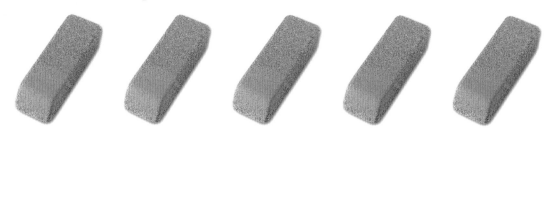

5 + 3 = ?

You have 5 erasers and find 3 more.

Count them all to find out how many you have.

0 1 2 3 4 5 6 7 8 9 10

Now try counting on to find out how many you have.

$$5 + 3 = ?$$

Start with 5 erasers.

Then count on 3 times.

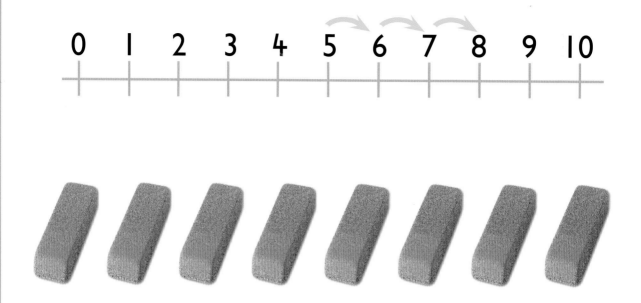

$$5 + 3 = 8$$

You have 8 erasers.

You can count them all or count on to find the answer.

Counting on is much quicker than counting them all!

Adding Balls

You have 6 balls and someone gives
you 4 more.

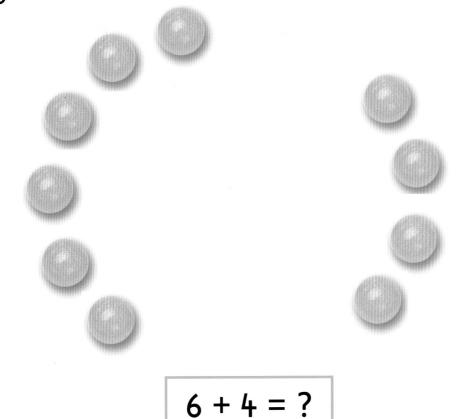

6 + 4 = ?

Count on to find out how many
you have.

0　1　2　3　4　5　6　7　8　9　10

Start with 6 and count on 4 times.

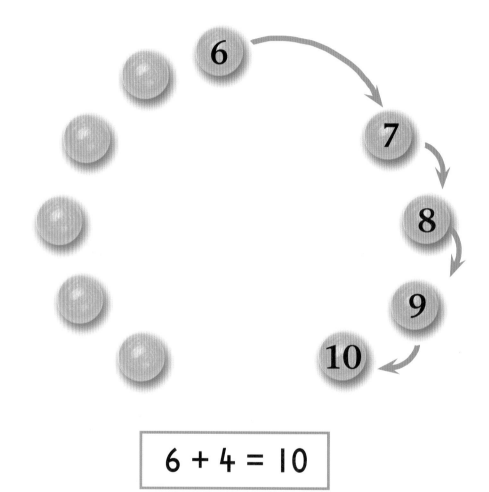

6 + 4 = 10

You have 10 balls.

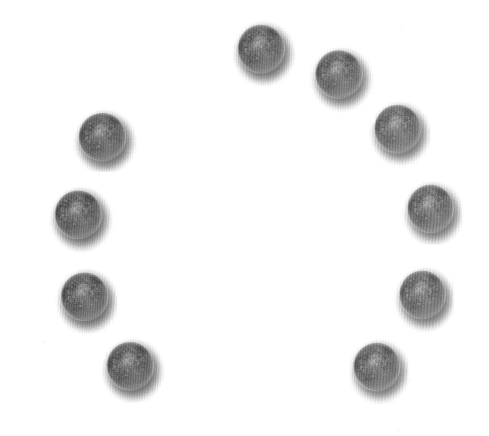

$$4 + 6 = \text{?}$$

What if you started with 4 balls and added 6 more?

Would you still have 10 balls?

Start at 4 and count on 6 times.

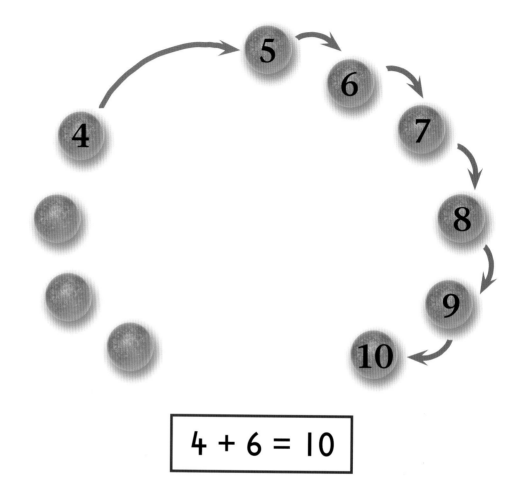

$$4 + 6 = 10$$

The total number of balls is the same.

You can start with 6 balls and add 4.

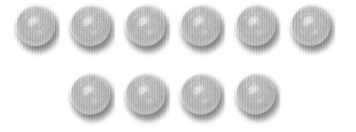

Or you can start with 4 balls and add 6.

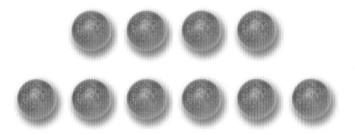

Either way, they combine to make the same number.

Practicing Adding

Adding is like putting things in a bag.

You can add things in any order.

You get the same number in the end.

$$5 + 2 = 7$$

Practice adding your own toys.

Adding becomes easier the more you practice!

Quiz

You have 6 shells.

Someone gives you 3 more.

Can you count on to find out how many shells you have now?

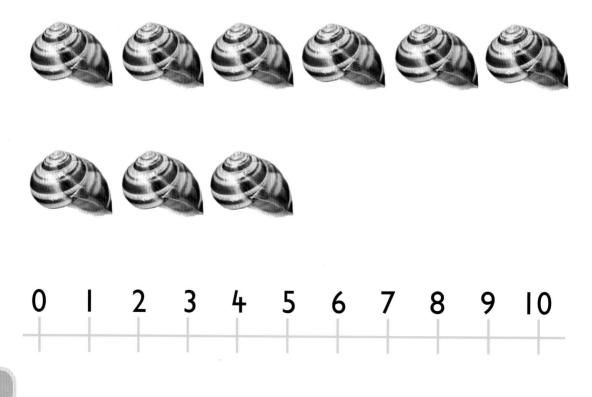

0   1   2   3   4   5   6   7   8   9   10

The Plus Sign

+   You use this sign to show that you are adding numbers.

$$3 + 2$$

When you add 3 and 2, you get 5.

=   You use the equals sign to show what 3 plus 2 is equal to.

$$3 + 2 = 5$$

Index

Answer to the quiz on page 22
You have 9 shells now.

Note to parents and teachers

Reading nonfiction texts for information is an important part of a child's literacy development. Readers can be encouraged to ask simple questions and then use the text to find the answers. Most chapters in this book begin with a question. Read the questions together. Look at the pictures. Talk about what the answer might be. Then read the text to find out if your predictions were correct. To develop readers' enquiry skills, encourage them to think of other questions they might ask about the topic. Discuss where you could find the answers. Assist children in using the contents page, picture glossary, and index to practice research skills and new vocabulary.